I0500614

GAO
Accountability * Integrity * Reliability

Highlights

Highlights of GAO-13-43, a report to congressional committees

AIR PASSENGER SCREENING

Transportation Security Administration Could Improve Complaint Processes

Why GAO Did This Study

TSA, which screens or oversees the screening of over 650 million air passengers per year, has processes for addressing complaints about air passengers' screening experience at checkpoints, but concerns have been raised about these processes. The Conference Report accompanying the Consolidated Appropriations Act, 2012, directed TSA to ensure the traveling public is aware of these processes and GAO to review TSA's policies and procedures for resolving passenger complaints. This report addresses the extent to which TSA has (1) policies and processes to guide the receipt of air passenger screening complaints and use of this information to monitor or enhance screening operations, (2) a consistent process for informing passengers about how to make complaints, and (3) complaint resolution processes that conform to independence standards. To address these objectives, GAO reviewed TSA documentation, analyzed complaint data from October 2009 through June 2012, and interviewed TSA officials from headquarters offices and six airports selected for type of security, among other things. The airport interviews are not generalizable but provide insights.

What GAO Recommends

GAO recommends that TSA, among other actions, establish (1) a consistent policy for receiving complaints, (2) a process to systematically analyze information on complaints from all mechanisms, and (3) a policy for informing passengers about the screening complaint processes and mechanisms to share best practices among airports. TSA concurred and is taking actions in response.

View GAO-13-43. For more information, contact Stephen M. Lord at (202) 512-4379 or lords@gao.gov.

What GAO Found

The Transportation Security Administration (TSA) receives thousands of air passenger screening complaints through five mechanisms, but does not have an agencywide policy or consistent processes to guide receipt and use of such information. For example, from October 2009 through June 2012, TSA received more than 39,000 screening complaints through its TSA Contact Center (TCC). However, the data from the five mechanisms do not reflect the full nature and extent of complaints because local TSA staff have discretion in implementing TSA's complaint processes, including how they receive and document complaints. For example, comment cards are used at four of the six airports GAO contacted, but TSA does not have a policy requiring that complaints submitted using the cards be tracked or reported centrally. A consistent policy to guide all TSA efforts to receive and document complaints would improve TSA's oversight of these activities and help ensure consistent implementation. TSA also uses TCC data to inform the public about air passenger screening complaints, monitor operational effectiveness of airport security checkpoints, and make changes as needed. However, TSA does not use data from its other four mechanisms, in part because the complaint categories differ, making data consolidation difficult. A process to systematically collect information from all mechanisms, including standard complaint categories, would better enable TSA to improve operations and customer service.

TSA has several methods to inform passengers about its complaint processes, but does not have an agencywide policy or mechanism to ensure consistent use of these methods among commercial airports. For example, TSA has developed standard signs, stickers, and customer comment cards that can be used at airport checkpoints to inform passengers about how to submit feedback to TSA; however, GAO found inconsistent use at the six airports it contacted. For example, two airports displayed customer comment cards at the checkpoint, while at two others the cards were provided upon request. Passengers may be reluctant to ask for such cards, however, according to TSA. TSA officials at four of the six airports also said that the agency could do more to share best practices for informing passengers about complaint processes. Policies for informing the public about complaint processes and mechanisms for sharing best practices among local TSA officials could help provide TSA reasonable assurance that these activities are being conducted consistently and help local TSA officials learn from one another about what practices work well.

TSA's complaint resolution processes do not fully conform to standards of independence to ensure that these processes are fair, impartial, and credible, but the agency is taking steps to improve independence. Specifically, TSA airport officials responsible for resolving air passenger complaints are generally in the same chain of command as TSA airport staff who are the subjects of the complaints. TSA is developing a new process that could help ensure greater independence by TSA units referring air passenger complaints directly to its Ombudsman Division and by providing passengers an independent avenue to make complaints to that division. TSA also plans to initiate a program by January 2013 in which selected TSA airport staff are to be trained as passenger advocates as a collateral duty. It is too early to assess the extent to which these initiatives will help mitigate possible concerns about independence.

_____ United States Government Accountability Office

Contents

Abbreviations

AFSD	Assistant Federal Security Director
ATSA	Aviation and Transportation Security Act
CSQIM	Customer Support and Quality Improvement Manager
DHS	U.S. Department of Homeland Security
FSD	Federal Security Director
GSA	U.S. General Services Administration
SPOT	Screening of Passengers by Observation Techniques
SPP	Screening Partnership Program
TCC	TSA Contact Center
TSA	Transportation Security Administration
TSO	Transportation Security Officer

United States Government Accountability Office
Washington, DC 20548

November 15, 2012

Congressional Committees

The Transportation Security Administration (TSA), established by the Aviation and Transportation Security Act (ATSA), provides for, or oversees the provision of, security screening operations at the nation's commercial airports.[1] In accordance with ATSA, all air passengers and their accessible property must pass through a security checkpoint and undergo screening before entering the sterile area of an airport.[2] TSA currently screens or oversees the screening of over 650 million air passengers per year at 752 security checkpoints at over 440 commercial airports nationwide. The December 2009 terrorist attempt to detonate an explosive device during an international flight bound for Detroit prompted TSA to implement changes to air passenger screening, including accelerating the nationwide deployment of Advanced Imaging Technology (commonly referred to as a full body scanner, which screens air passengers for weapons, explosives, and other objects concealed under layers of clothing) and introducing enhanced pat-down procedures to screen air passengers who, for example, opt out of Advanced Imaging Technology-based screening. Air passenger screening complaints reflect a wide range of concerns, including those related to the use of Advanced Imaging Technology and concerns about enhanced pat-down procedures

---

[1]See Pub. L. No. 107-71, 115 Stat. 597 (2001). For this report, we use the term "air passengers" to include ticketed passengers, individuals accompanying ticketed passengers, airline crew members, and any other individuals who pass through security checkpoints employing TSA-approved screening procedures at TSA-regulated airports. In this report, we use the term "commercial airports" to refer to all TSA-regulated airports operating under TSA-approved security programs in accordance with 49 C.F.R. pt. 1542 and at which TSA or private sector screeners who are subject to TSA oversight screen air passengers and their property.

[2]The sterile area is that portion of an airport specified in the airport security program that provides passengers access to boarding aircraft and to which the access generally is controlled through the screening of persons and property. See 49 C.F.R. § 1540.5.

being unnecessarily intrusive.[3] TSA has various processes for receiving and resolving complaints that air passengers may have about their screening experience at security checkpoints; however, public concerns have been raised about these processes.

The Conference Report accompanying the Consolidated Appropriations Act, 2012, directed TSA to make every effort to ensure that members of the traveling public are aware of the procedures and processes for making complaints about air passenger screening.[4] The Conference Report also directed that we review TSA's policies and procedures for resolving passenger complaints, including an assessment of organizational independence. In response, this report addresses the following questions: (1) To what extent does TSA have policies and processes in place to guide the receipt of air passenger screening complaints and use this information to monitor or enhance screening operations? (2) To what extent does TSA have a consistent process for informing air passengers about how to make screening complaints? (3) To what extent does TSA have complaint resolution processes that conform to standards of independence to ensure that these processes are fair, impartial, and credible?

To address the first objective, we reviewed TSA documentation on the processes for receiving and documenting complaints at different offices within TSA headquarters and locally at airports. We also obtained documentation on TSA's use of air passenger screening complaints, such as complaint data that TSA provides to the U.S. Department of Transportation for publication in its monthly *Air Travel Consumer Report*. We interviewed officials from TSA, the U.S. Department of Homeland Security (DHS), and a nonprobability sample of eight aviation industry

---

[3]For purposes of this review, "screening complaints" include any documented expression of dissatisfaction or request for redress that TSA or its contractors receive orally (and that is subsequently documented) or in writing at the airport checkpoints or through mail, e-mail, telephone, agency websites, or other means, related to agency and contractor screening systems, procedures, and staff deployed at airport security checkpoints. Complaints about prescreening of air passengers through the Department of Homeland Security's Traveler Redress Inquiry Program, complaints about screening of checked baggage, and air passenger claims for lost, stolen, and damaged property are not included in our scope.

[4]See H.R. Rep. No. 112-331, at 975 (2011) (accompanying H.R. 2055, 112th Cong. (1st Sess. 2011), enacted as the Consolidated Appropriations Act, 2012, Pub. L. No. 112-74, 125 Stat. 786 (2011)).

groups to obtain their perspectives on TSA's processes for receiving and documenting air passenger screening complaints and for using this information to monitor or enhance screening operations.[5] The views of these industry groups are not generalizable to all members of the aviation industry but provided us with additional perspective and insights. The groups were selected to include organizations representing airlines, airports, travel agencies, and travelers, among others. In addition, we interviewed officials from the U.S. Department of Transportation's Aviation Consumer Protection Division. We also obtained and analyzed air passenger screening complaint data from October 2009 through June 2012 from four TSA headquarters units.[6] We selected October 2009 as the starting point because it was the first month of the fiscal year that included the December 2009 terrorist attempt to detonate an explosive device during an international flight bound for Detroit, which prompted TSA to implement changes to its air passenger screening operations. In addition, we obtained and analyzed air passenger screening complaint data from April 2011 through June 2012 from a database TSA uses to document screening complaints collected through TSA's Talk to TSA web-based portal.[7] This database became operational in April 2011, according to TSA officials. On the basis of information from and discussions with TSA officials related to the controls in place to maintain the integrity of TSA's complaint data, we determined that the data from each database were sufficiently reliable for our purposes.

In addition, we selected a nonprobability sample of six airports—including one airport participating in TSA's Screening Partnership Program (SPP)—at which to interview TSA airport officials (and contractors' representatives) about their processes for receiving and documenting air

---

[5]The TSA offices include the following: Office of Security Operations; Office of Civil Rights & Liberties, Ombudsman, and Traveler Engagement; Office of the Executive Secretariat; Office of Public Affairs; Office of Inspections; and Office of Legislative Affairs. The DHS offices include the Office of Civil Rights & Civil Liberties, the Privacy Office, and the Office of the Inspector General. The aviation industry groups include Airlines for America; Airports Council International-North America; American Association of Airport Executives; Business Travel Coalition, Inc.; FlyersRights.Org; Global Business Travel Association; Regional Airline Association; and U.S. Travel Association.

[6]These units are the TSA Contact Center Branch, the Office of the Executive Secretariat, the Disability Branch, and the Multicultural Branch.

[7]This portal, which resides on TSA's website, e-mails screening complaint information directly to designated TSA airport staff.

passenger screening complaints and for using this information to inform screening operations and improve customer service.[8] We also obtained supporting documentation and data from officials at these six airports. We selected these airports based on airport security category[9] and types of screening equipment and initiatives at the airports, such as the use of Advanced Imaging Technology and TSA's enhanced behavior detection pilot program.[10] The selected airports are located in the Washington, D.C.; Detroit; and Los Angeles metropolitan areas; and the SPP airport is located in the San Francisco metropolitan area. We visited and observed security checkpoints at four of the airports.[11] At the five airports where TSA performs the screening function, we interviewed TSA Federal Security Director (FSD) staff responsible for screening and customer service, such as TSA screening supervisors and managers and TSA Customer Support Managers. At the SPP airport, we interviewed TSA FSD staff responsible for customer service and contractor officials responsible for screening. While the information gathered from the interviews cannot be generalized to all commercial airports, it provided important perspective to our analysis of air passenger screening complaint processes, which is focused on airports at which TSA staff conduct screening. At the TSA headquarters units and airports we

---

[8]In general, TSA employees (referred to as Transportation Security Officers) perform the screening function at the nation's commercial airports. Through SPP, however, employees of private companies under contract to TSA perform the screening function, following the same screening procedures at checkpoints used by Transportation Security Officers. See 49 U.S.C. § 44920. Sixteen airports currently participate in SPP, with six additional airports approved in fiscal year 2012 for participation in the program. We are currently conducting a separate review of SPP and plan to report on the results of this work later this year.

[9]TSA classifies the nation's commercial airports into one of five categories (X, I, II, III, and IV) based on various factors such as the number of takeoffs and landings annually, the extent of passenger screening at the airport, and other security considerations. In general, category X airports have the largest number of passenger boardings and category IV airports have the smallest.

[10]We have ongoing work reviewing TSA's Screening of Passengers by Observation Techniques (SPOT) program and its enhanced behavior detection pilot program and plan to report the results of this work in early 2013. The SPOT program is a behavior observation and analysis program designed to provide the TSA Behavior Detection Officers who interact with air passengers at the security checkpoints with a means of identifying persons who pose or may pose potential transportation security risks by focusing on behaviors indicative of high levels of stress, fear, or deception.

[11]We interviewed staff from the other two airports, including the SPP airport, by phone, and therefore did not visit checkpoints at those airports.

interviewed, we compared TSA's processes for receiving and documenting air passenger screening complaints and for using the information to monitor and enhance screening operations and improve customer service against *Standards for Internal Control in the Federal Government.*[12]

To address the second objective, we reviewed TSA documentation on how the agency informs passengers about its air passenger complaint processes, such as agency guidance, website information, comment cards, and signs. We also interviewed officials at TSA and the selected airports about the agency's methods for informing air passengers about TSA's processes for making screening complaints (and about TSA's contractor's complaint processes). We compared these methods with *Standards for Internal Control in the Federal Government.*[13]

To address the third objective, we obtained and analyzed TSA guidance for resolving air passenger screening complaints, as well as the organizational structure of TSA offices responsible for resolving screening complaints. We compared this information with pertinent criteria from *Standards for Internal Control in the Federal Government* and other standards for independence, such as ombudsman standards for governmental organizations,[14] to assess the extent to which TSA's screening complaint resolution processes are independent from those responsible for conducting screening at airport checkpoints so as to ensure that these processes are fair, impartial, and credible. We interviewed TSA officials responsible for resolving screening complaints, including customer support managers at the selected airports, as well as aviation industry group representatives. We also interviewed TSA officials about the agency's plans for creating an external ombudsman function to resolve screening complaints.

We conducted this performance audit from February 2012 to November 2012 in accordance with generally accepted government auditing

---

[12]GAO, *Standards for Internal Control in the Federal Government*, GAO/AIMD-00-21.3.1 (Washington, D.C.: November 1999).

[13]GAO/AIMD-00-21.3.1.

[14]GAO/AIMD-00-21.3.1; American Bar Association, *Revised Standards for the Establishment and Operation of Ombuds Offices* (February 2004); and United States Ombudsman Association, *Governmental Ombudsman Standards*, (Dayton, OH: October 2003).

standards. Those standards require that we plan and perform the audit to obtain sufficient, appropriate evidence to provide a reasonable basis for our findings and conclusions based on our audit objectives. We believe that the evidence obtained provides a reasonable basis for our findings and conclusions based on our audit objectives.

Background

Roles and Responsibilities for Receiving and Addressing Screening Complaints

TSA has various processes for receiving and addressing air passenger complaints about the screening systems, procedures, and personnel at airport security checkpoints.[15] Specifically, several TSA headquarters units and local TSA airport staff have responsibility and processes for receiving and addressing these complaints, and, if necessary, referring these complaints to other TSA offices for resolution.[16] Figure 1 depicts the four primary TSA headquarters units and the local TSA airport staff who are responsible for receiving and addressing air passenger screening complaints.[17]

---

[15]Complaint processes at the airport level differ somewhat between airports at which TSA has direct responsibility for screening and SPP airports. For example, while screeners at both types of airports follow the same standard operating procedures for screening air passengers, the contractor responsible for screening at the SPP airport also has general responsibility for addressing complaints submitted to the contractor at the checkpoint, while TSA staff at that airport are generally responsible for addressing complaints submitted through TSA's Contact Center or the Talk to TSA web-based portal. For the purposes of this report, we are referring to airports at which TSA has direct responsibility for screening in discussions of roles, responsibilities, and processes for addressing complaints at the airport level.

[16]When airport authorities, airlines, and other federal agencies, such as the U.S. Department of Transportation, receive air passenger screening complaints, they typically refer them to TSA, according to officials that we contacted at these entities.

[17]Other TSA headquarters offices can also play a role in addressing screening complaints. For instance, the Office of Legislative Affairs handles congressional inquiries and correspondence that relate to screening complaints. As we discuss later in this report, the TSA Ombudsman is working on an initiative to begin addressing screening complaints. In addition, we discussed the TSA Contact Center's customer service efforts in GAO, *Managing for Results: Opportunities to Strengthen Agencies' Customer Service Efforts*, GAO-11-44 (Washington, D.C.: Oct. 27, 2010).

Figure 1: TSA Headquarters Units and Local TSA Airport Staff Responsible for Receiving and Addressing Air Passenger Screening Complaints

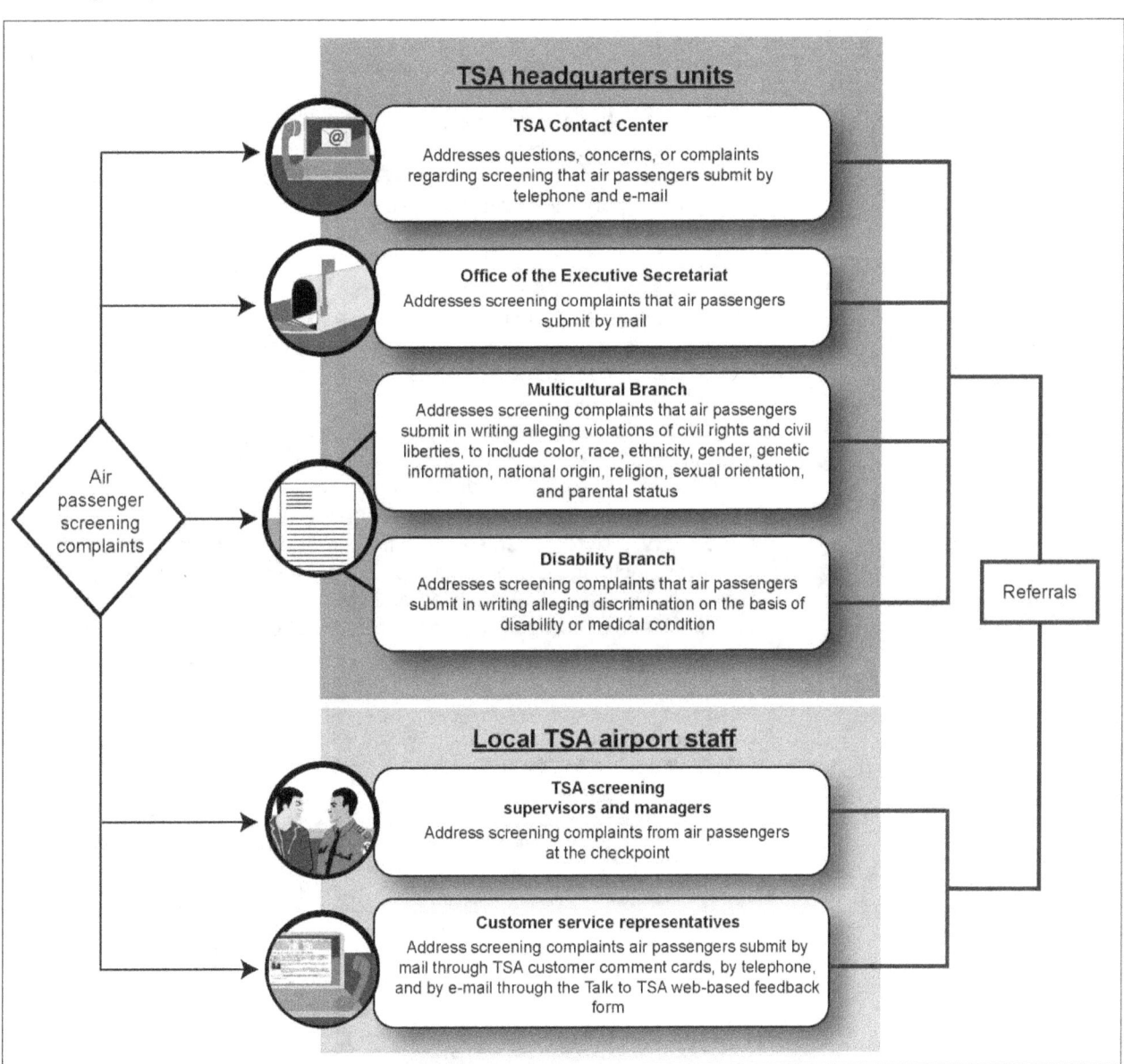

Source: GAO analysis of TSA information.

Note: According to TSA officials, if air passengers cannot submit screening complaints in writing because of disability, medical condition, or language barrier, the Disability and Multicultural Branches will accept their complaints by telephone or other means and then create written versions of the complaints for processing.

As highlighted in figure 1, the TSA Contact Center (TCC) receives, documents, and helps resolve screening complaints that air passengers make by telephone and e-mail. The TCC is TSA's primary point of contact for collecting, documenting, and responding to public questions, concerns, or complaints regarding TSA security policies, procedures, and programs; reports and claims of lost, stolen, or damaged items; and employment issues.[18]

At the local level, TSA screening supervisors and managers oversee screening systems, procedures, and Transportation Security Officers at the airport security checkpoints and are responsible for receiving and addressing complaints that air passengers orally submit as they proceed through the checkpoints.[19] TSA customer service representatives are responsible for receiving and addressing screening complaints that air passengers make through customer comment cards, telephone calls, or a Talk to TSA web-based feedback form.[20] (See an example of a customer comment card in fig. 2.) The customer service representatives serve as the primary TSA representatives at the airports for all customer service initiatives, including customer complaint resolution activities. Some of these representatives are Customer Support Managers, which are full-time positions at category X airports and an ancillary duty of the FSD or

[18]The TCC addresses inquiries from air passengers on claims for damaged, lost, or stolen property and advises these passengers on how to file a claim when appropriate. However, it is the Claims Management Branch and the Office of the Chief Counsel that resolve these claims.

[19]These officials include Lead and Supervisory Transportation Security Officers as well as Transportation Security Managers. At SPP airports, they include supervisory contractor officials. FSDs and Assistant Federal Security Directors are responsible for overseeing TSA security programs at all commercial airports. According to the Assistant Administrator of TSA's Office of Civil Rights & Liberties, Ombudsman and Traveler Engagement, the agency is working on an initiative under which an unspecified number of TSA staff will receive training as "passenger advocates" and begin working in this capacity to address air passenger complaints at security checkpoints by January 2013.

[20]According to TSA officials, air passengers may submit other written screening complaints to customer service representatives by mail using the information for mailing customer comment cards. Also, air passengers may submit screening complaints to these representatives by e-mail, although the e-mail contact information for these representatives is not always provided in the customer comment cards.

screener staff at other commercial airports.[21] Customer Support Managers work in conjunction with other FSD staff to resolve customer complaints and communicate the status and resolution of complaints to air passengers. They are also responsible for ensuring security procedures and practices are consistently and effectively communicated to air passengers, to the extent permitted by law and regulation.[22]

---

[21]The official title for this position is Customer Support and Quality Improvement Manager (CSQIM) but it is commonly referred to as Customer Support Manager. TSA had 115 Customer Support Managers as of October 2012.

[22]In addition to Customer Support Managers, some airports may also have TSA Stakeholder Relations Managers, who deal primarily with airlines, local law enforcement, and airport tenants. The Stakeholder Relations Manager is not directly tied to customer service, but depending on the airport, may have a customer support role, according to TSA and airport officials we interviewed. The type and number of positions as well as the reporting structure of these positions varies at each airport based on the size of the airport and passenger numbers, according to TSA officials.

Figure 2: Example of TSA Customer Comment Card

TSA CUSTOMER COMMENT CARD

Transportation
Security
Administration

The Transportation Security Administration (TSA) pledges to ensure that your experience at the security checkpoint is expedient and customer-friendly. Please help us to meet these goals by telling us about your screening experience. Suggestions, compliments and complaints are welcomed and encouraged.

If you want to provide feedback at the airport:
- Ask to speak with a TSA screening supervisor or manager, or
- Contact the TSA customer service representative at the airport, or
- **Complete the back of this card** and return it to a TSA supervisor or manager or place in drop-box.

You may also contact TSA by:
- Calling the TSA Contact Center toll-free at 1-866-289-9673 (voice), (800) 877-8339 (TTY/TTD), or
- Sending an e-mail message: TSA-ContactCenter@dhs.gov.
- Mailing this card: (Insert Local Address HERE)

It would be helpful to provide the following information: airport and terminal, date and time of your trip, airline and flight number, name and badge number of TSA employees you spoke with, and any other pertinent information.

www.tsa.gov

(OVER)

Transportation
Security
Administration

Help us improve our customer service by completing and returning this card to a TSA drop-box or to a TSA supervisor or manager.

Date: _____ Time: _____ Airport: _____

Date/Time of Travel: _____ Airline & flight number: _____

Checkpoint/area of airport:_____TSA Employee(if known): _____

COMPLIMENT/COMPLAINT(summarize):_____

_____

_____

_____

_____

_____

Passenger's Name: (optional, so we can follow-up with you) _____

(Optional) Phone number _____ e-mail: _____

NOTE: If you wish to seek payment from TSA for damaged or missing items, you must file a claim on-line at www.tsa.gov or through the TSA Contact Center at *1-866-289-9673*.

Collection of this information is made under 49 U.S.C.114(e) & (f). Providing this information is **voluntary**. TSA will use the information to improve customer service and may share it with airport operators for this purpose. For more information, please consult DHS/TSA 006 Correspondence and Matters Tracking Records. It will take no more that 5 minutes to complete this form. An agency may not conduct or sponsor, and a person is not required to respond to, a collection of information unless it displays a valid OMB control number. The control number assigned to this collection is **OMB 1652-0039, which expires 4/30/2014.** Send comments regarding this burden estimate or any other aspect of this collection of information including suggestions for reducing this burden to TSA/ 601 S. 12th Street, Arlington, VA 22202. **ATTN: PRA 1652-0030.**

Source: TSA.

Complaint Referral and Resolution

TSA has an operations directive that specifies roles, responsibilities, and time frames for resolving and responding to screening complaints that air passengers submit to the TCC and FSD staff.[23] This directive does not apply to complaints received through other mechanisms, as we discuss later in this report. The agency has also given TSA headquarters units and FSDs discretion in addressing these complaints at airports under their jurisdiction, according to TSA officials. This operations directive provides instructions for processing public inquiries, including air passenger screening complaints, received by the TCC and FSD staff.[24] The directive indicates that inquiries received by the TCC will be answered by the TCC or will be forwarded to the appropriate FSD staff for response, and that inquiries received by FSD staff will be answered by FSD staff or will be forwarded to the TCC for response. In addition, the operations directive provides several time frames for responding to complaints. For example, TSA should respond within 48 hours for e-mail inquiries addressed by the TCC, and within 72 hours for telephone inquiries addressed by the TCC.

Overall, upon receiving a complaint, TSA headquarters units and local TSA airport staff may address the complaint directly or refer it to other offices for review and resolution after determining which one has the necessary expertise and knowledge to address the alleged incident. For example, according to TSA officials, if an air passenger submits the complaint through the TCC, TCC staff attempt to resolve it by providing a response to the air passenger using pertinent template language that explains TSA policy and screening procedures. Alternatively, the TCC may refer screening complaints for resolution to other TSA headquarters offices, depending on the specific allegation. For example, complaints alleging discrimination on the basis of a disability or medical condition are

---

[23]See *TSA Operations Directive: Processing Inquiries Received by the TSA Contact Center, TSA Claims Management Office, and Federal Security Director Staffs*, OD-400-5-1A, September 15, 2005.

[24]As defined in the operational directive, an inquiry is defined as any communication, letter mail, facsimile, electronic mail, or telephone call received by the TCC or by FSD staff that requires a response. To complement this operations directive, TSA staff at one of the six airports that we contacted during our review had additional written instructions for processing public inquiries, such as air passenger screening complaints.

GAO-13-43 Air Passenger Screening Complaints

referred to the Disability Branch.[25] Also, the TCC may forward complaints about customer service to the customer service representative at the airport identified in the complaint for investigation and resolution.[26] Alternatively, if an air passenger submits a complaint directly to TSA staff at the airport, it is the responsibility of these staff members to investigate and resolve the complaint or, if necessary, refer it to TSA units at headquarters, such as the Disability Branch. For example, according to TSA officials, if an air passenger makes a complaint in person at the checkpoint, TSA supervisors and managers are to attempt to resolve the complaint at the checkpoint before the situation escalates.

Regardless of whether a complaint is initially received by a TSA headquarters unit or at the airport at which the incident took place, according to TSA officials, local TSA airport officials generally conduct most follow-up investigations since they are well placed to collect additional airport-specific information and interview local staff. However, specific actions taken to investigate and resolve complaints vary by airport. For example, customer service representatives may be involved in reviewing screening complaints, obtaining additional information from the air passengers to determine when and where the incident took place, and reviewing video footage of the incident to help identify additional details of the incident, such as the identity of the screener(s) who may have been involved in the incident and what had actually happened during the incident. If the situation warrants it, the customer service representative may forward the complaint as well as the video footage to the TSA screening supervisor or manager for additional review and action. The supervisor or manager may review the video footage and obtain a statement from the screener to determine what happened during the incident and the extent to which the screener may have been at fault—for example, whether the screener violated TSA standard operating

---

[25]The Disability and Multicultural Branches work with DHS's Office of Civil Rights & Civil Liberties in addressing some air passenger screening complaints. For example, the office generally refers screening complaints that it receives from air passengers to the branches for resolution, according to TSA officials. Also, the office may offer technical assistance to the branches when handling screening complaints. In the case of disability screening complaints, according to TSA officials, the Disability Branch provides weekly information on these complaints to this office, and air passengers can appeal the decisions of the Disability Branch to this office.

[26]For the purpose of this report, "investigation" refers to actions taken to gather information needed to resolve a complaint, and "complaint investigator" refers to the person responsible for gathering that information.

procedures, or behaved unprofessionally or inappropriately toward the air passenger.

Depending on the nature and severity of the allegation, TSA airport staff may also elevate the complaint and evidence to the airport's Assistant Federal Security Director (AFSD) for Screening or to TSA headquarters units, such as the Disability Branch or the Office of Inspections, for formal investigation.[27] If the investigation were to find fault with the screener, the screener's supervisor or manager is to determine the corrective action to be taken.[28] Corrective actions specified in TSA's guidance range from mandating the screener to take additional training to correct the behavior to terminating the screener's employment for multiple repeat offenses or single egregious actions, such as theft of air passenger property.[29] Following the outcome of the investigation and any resulting corrective actions, the TSA headquarters unit or the FSD or his/her staff, such as a customer service representative, is to communicate the status of the resolution to the air passenger—such as by reiterating that TSA procedures were followed or by issuing an apology and informing the air passenger that corrective actions were taken.

---

[27]According to officials from the Office of Inspections, their office has not conducted formal investigations of air passenger screening complaints.

[28]We previously reported that complaint resolution processes in federal agencies should help ensure that the subjects of complaints receive appropriate training or disciplinary action, when necessary, in order to help prevent a problem from occurring again. GAO, *Crime Victims' Rights Act: Increasing Awareness, Modifying the Complaint Process, and Enhancing Compliance Monitoring Will Improve Implementation of the Act*, GAO-09-54 (Washington, D.C.: Dec. 15, 2008).

[29]TSA, *Guidelines on Using the Table of Offenses and Penalties for Appropriate Discipline for Common Offenses*, September 26, 2011. The Disability and Multicultural Branches can also recommend that screeners receive additional training, if appropriate.

Lack of an Agencywide Policy, Consistent Processes, and Agency Focal Point Limits TSA's Ability to Receive and Use Complaint Information

TSA's five centralized mechanisms for receiving air passenger screening complaints provide the agency with a significant amount of information it can use to monitor or enhance screening operations. However, TSA does not have agencywide policy, consistent processes, or an agency focal point to guide the receipt of these complaints or to use complaint information to inform management about the nature and extent of the screening complaints to help improve screening operations and customer service.

Five Mechanisms Receive Thousands of Air Passenger Complaints

TSA receives and documents screening complaints that air passengers submit through four headquarters units—the TCC, the Executive Secretariat, the Multicultural Branch, and the Disability Branch—as well as the Talk to TSA web-based feedback mechanism, which e-mails the screening complaint information directly to designated TSA airport staff. As shown in figure 3, the number of complaints submitted through these mechanisms fluctuated somewhat from October 2009 through June 2012. The major exception was a very large increase in the number of complaints submitted to three mechanisms in November and December 2010, which may be attributed to several factors, including a November 2010 public opt-out campaign reported by the media to protest the use of Advanced Imaging Technology and enhanced pat-down procedures for screening air passengers.

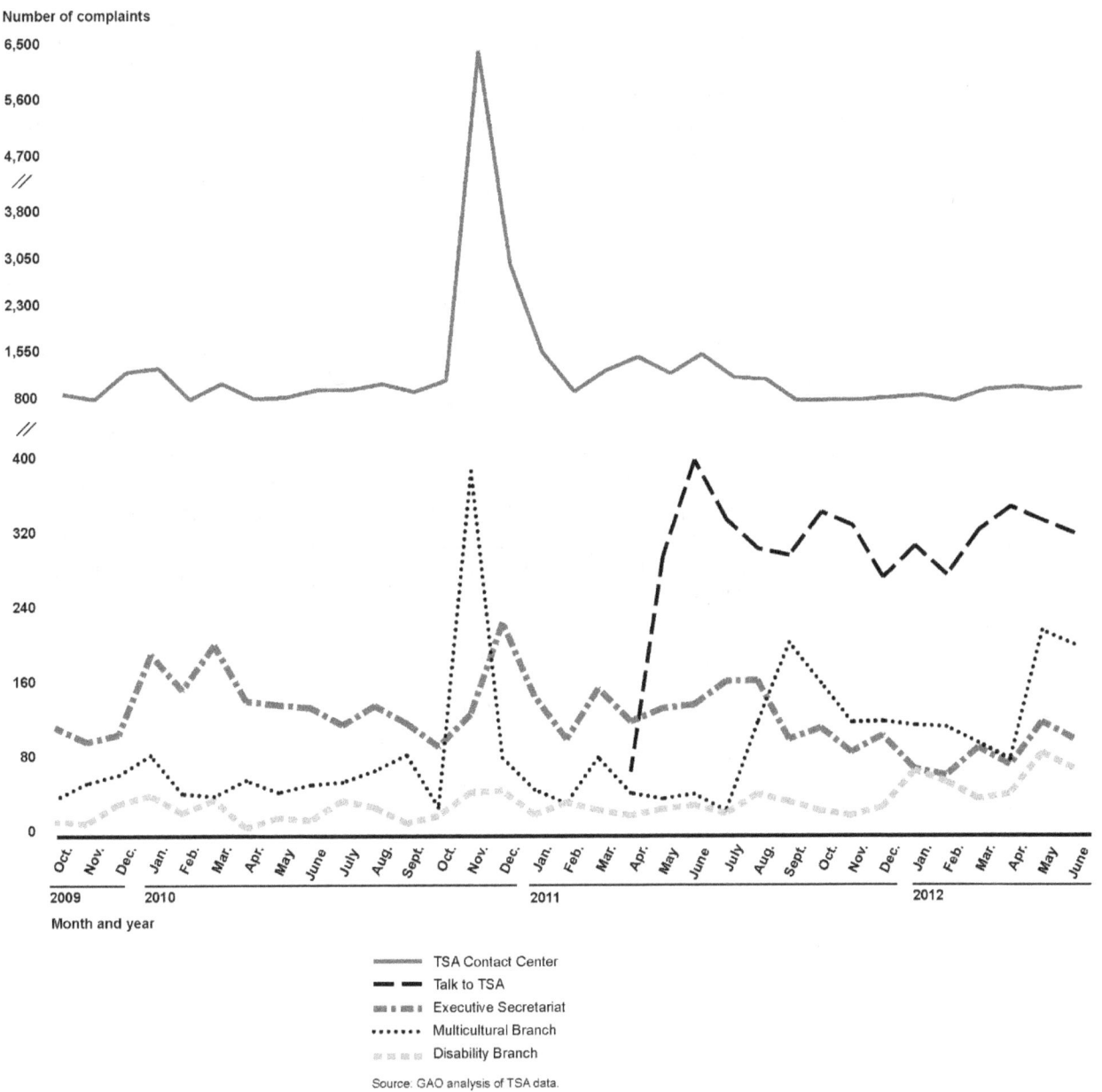

Figure 3: Numbers of Monthly Air Passenger Screening Complaints That TSA Received from October 2009 through June 2012

Number of complaints

Month and year

TSA Contact Center
Talk to TSA
Executive Secretariat
Multicultural Branch
Disability Branch

Source: GAO analysis of TSA data.

GAO-13-43 Air Passenger Screening Complaints

The volume of complaints that TSA received through each of its five main mechanisms varied from October 2009 through June 2012. Also, because these mechanisms use different categories for screening complaints and have different capabilities for data analysis, we were not able to combine the data from these mechanisms to discuss overall patterns and trends in volume or categories of complaints. A discussion of complaint information in each mechanism follows.

The TCC received the bulk of the air passenger screening complaints that the agency documented during this time period. Using TCC data, TSA has reported that it receives about 750,000 public inquiries annually through the TCC and that 8 percent of these inquiries involve air passenger complaints (including complaints about screening). As noted below, however, this information does not include complaint data from other TSA complaint mechanisms. Specifically, the TCC received a total of 39,616 screening complaints that air passengers submitted by e-mail and telephone from October 2009 through June 2012. The TCC divides screening complaints into seven main categories, five having multiple subcategories. Figure 4 shows the total numbers of screening complaints by the seven main TCC categories, such as 17,153 complaints about pat-down procedures.

Figure 4: Total Numbers of Air Passenger Screening Complaints That the TCC Received from October 2009 through June 2012, by Category

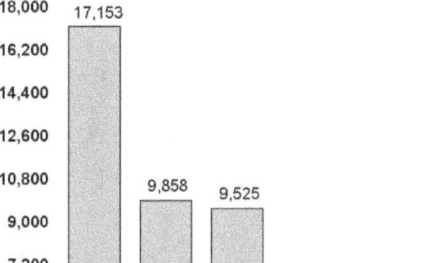

Number of complaints

Source: GAO analysis of TSA data.

Note: Five of the seven main categories in the TCC database contain multiple subcategories.

Figure 5 depicts the numbers of screening complaints that the TCC received from October 2009 through June 2012 by the four main TCC categories having the most complaints. As shown in figure 5, the numbers of screening complaints in these four categories remained relatively stable over this period. The major exception was a very large increase in the number of complaints about pat-down procedures in November and December 2010 and continuing periods of a relatively higher level of pat-down complaints through September 2011. As mentioned before, this increase in complaints may be attributed to several factors, including the November 2010 public opt-out campaign reported by the media to protest the use of Advanced Imaging Technology and enhanced pat-down procedures for screening air passengers.

GAO-13-43 Air Passenger Screening Complaints

Figure 5: Numbers of Air Passenger Screening Complaints That the TCC Received from October 2009 through June 2012, by Category (Four Largest Categories)

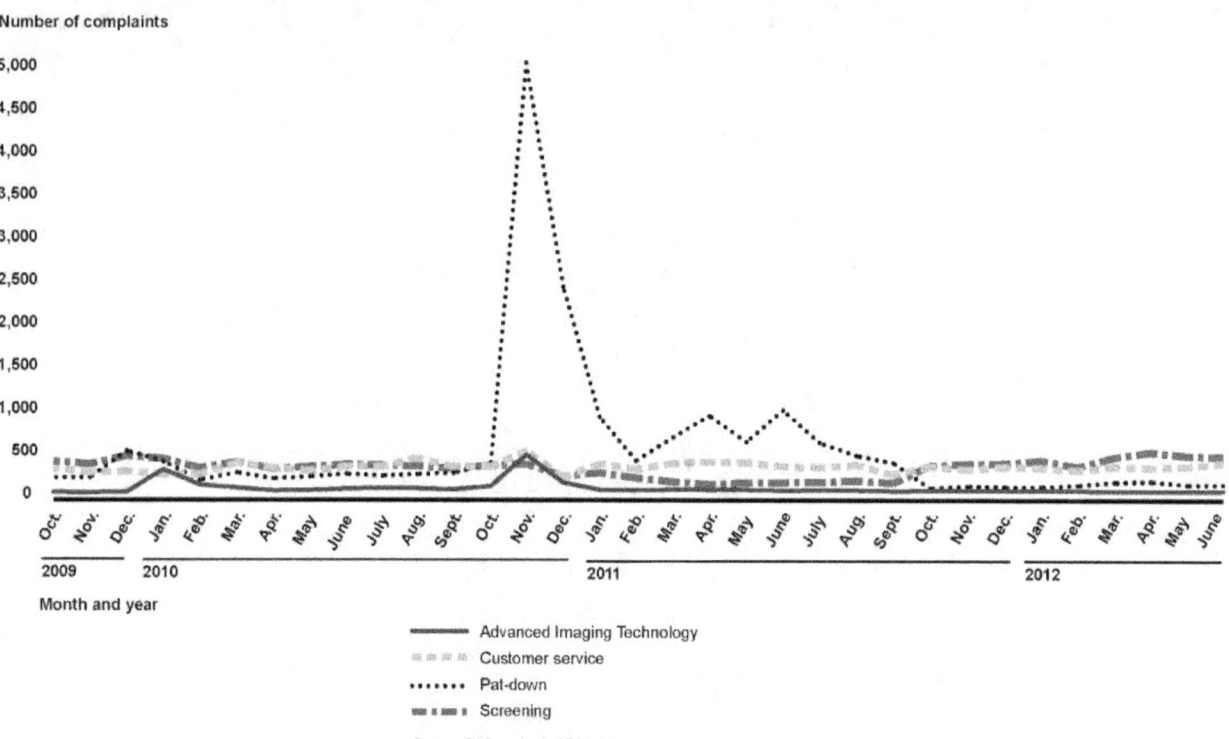

Number of complaints

----- Advanced Imaging Technology
▦ ▦ ▦ ▦ Customer service
•••••• Pat-down
▬ ▪ ▬ ▪ Screening

Source: GAO analysis of TSA data.

The Office of the Executive Secretariat received 4,011 complaints that air passengers submitted by mail.[30] For instance, these complaints include screening complaints related to, among other issues, Advanced Imaging Technology and enhanced pat-down procedures.[31]

---

[30]According to officials in this office, the Executive Secretariat database does not have the capability to differentiate between screening and nonscreening-related complaints based on the information it has on complaint subject categories.

[31]Although this database and the TCC database have certain categories with similar or identical names, other categories are specific to each database. For example, the Executive Secretariat database includes a category for inappropriate screening, while this type of complaint could be categorized in the TCC database as inconsistent screening or as screening process, among other categories.

The Multicultural Branch received 2,899 written screening complaints alleging violations of civil rights and civil liberties, 469 of which it processed as cases.[32] Figure 6 shows the number of cases, by 11 categories, that the branch processed, such as 141 cases related to allegations of discrimination based on race or ethnicity.

Figure 6: Numbers of Air Passenger Screening Complaints That the Multicultural Branch Processed as Cases from October 2009 through June 2012, by Category

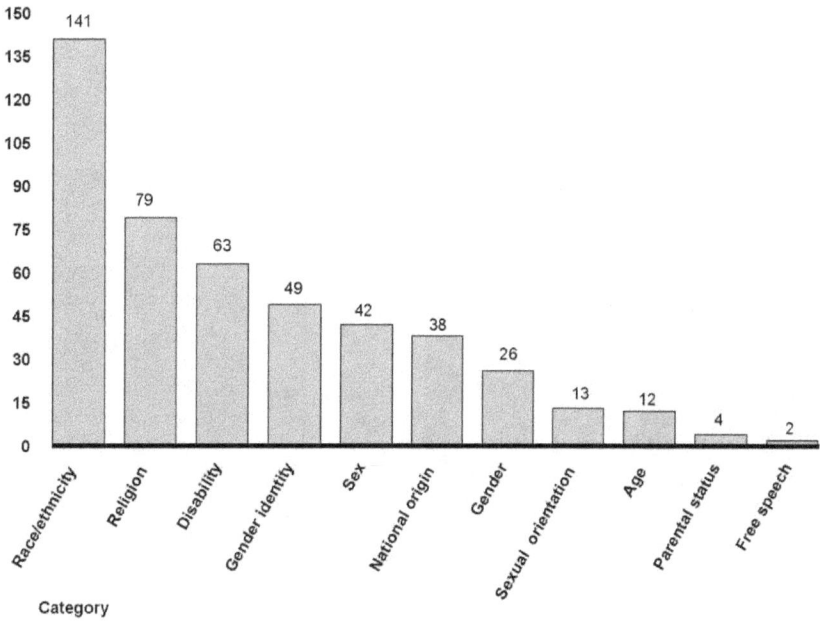

Source: GAO analysis of TSA data.

Note: The TCC database has a category for civil rights complaints, but its subcategories are not directly comparable with the Multicultural Branch categories. For example, TCC includes subcategories for harassment, perceived discrimination, and perceived racial profiling, among others.

---

[32]According to TSA officials, the branch refers screening complaints that it does not process as cases to other TSA units. The Multicultural Branch does not record categories for the complaints that it does not process as cases, so we did not include them in figure 6.

GAO-13-43 Air Passenger Screening Complaints

The Disability Branch received 920 written screening complaints alleging discrimination on the basis of disability and medical condition. From these, the branch processed 1,233 cases.[33] Figure 7 shows the number of cases, by 27 categories, that the branch processed, such as 201 cases related to inappropriate screening.

---

[33]If the screening complaint submitted by an air passenger includes complaints that fall under different categories of disabilities, the branch would process each one of them as a separate case. Thus, there are more cases processed than complaints received by the Disability Branch from October 2009 through June 2012.

Figure 7: Numbers of Air Passenger Screening Complaints That the Disability Branch Processed as Cases from October 2009 through June 2012, by Category

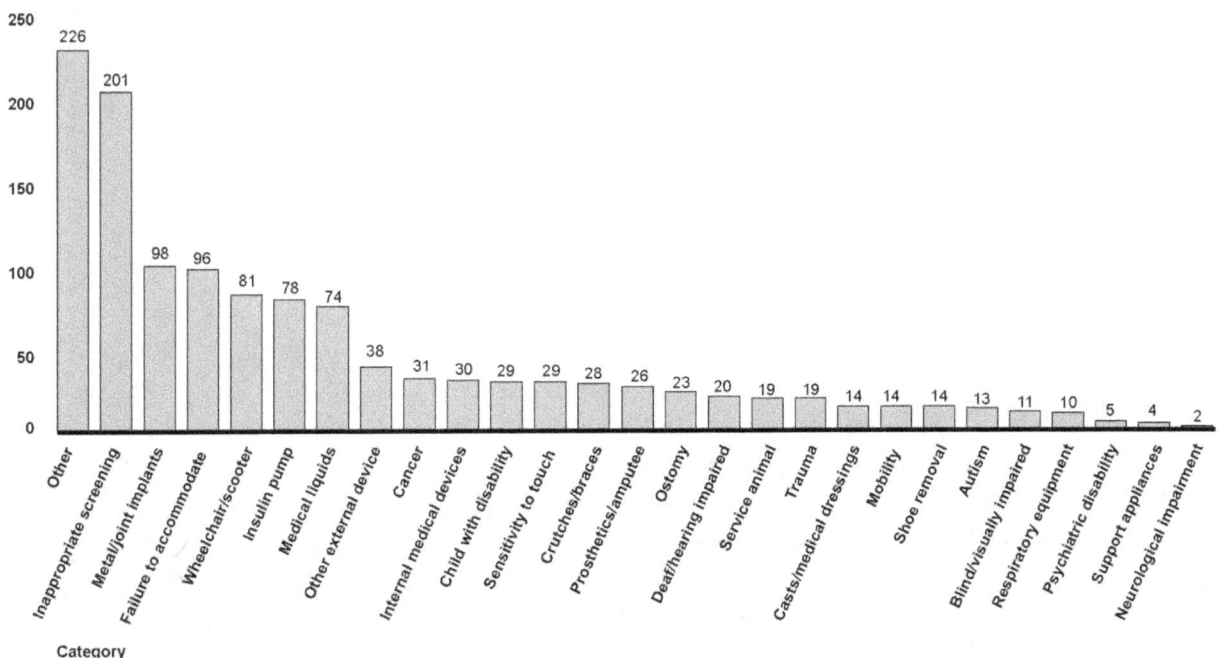

Source: GAO analysis of TSA data.

Note: The TCC database has a category for disability complaints, but its subcategories for these complaints are not directly comparable with the Disability Branch categories. For example, the TCC database includes a subcategory for diabetes, while the Disability Branch has a category for insulin pumps. Also, more than half of the screening cases in the "Other" category are from fiscal year 2010 because for that year the database did not have enough categories defined, according to TSA officials. The Disability Branch added additional categories to the database for fiscal year 2012 to avoid overusing the "Other" category.

The Talk to TSA web-based mechanism received 4,506 air passenger screening complaints from April 2011 through June 2012. When submitting complaints through this mechanism, air passengers can select up to five complaint categories from a list of 20 possible categories. Figure 8 shows the number of screening complaints by 20 categories that the branch received, such as 1,512 complaints about the professionalism of TSA staff during the screening process.[34]

Figure 8: Numbers of Air Passenger Screening Complaints That Talk to TSA Received from April 2011 through June 2012, by Category

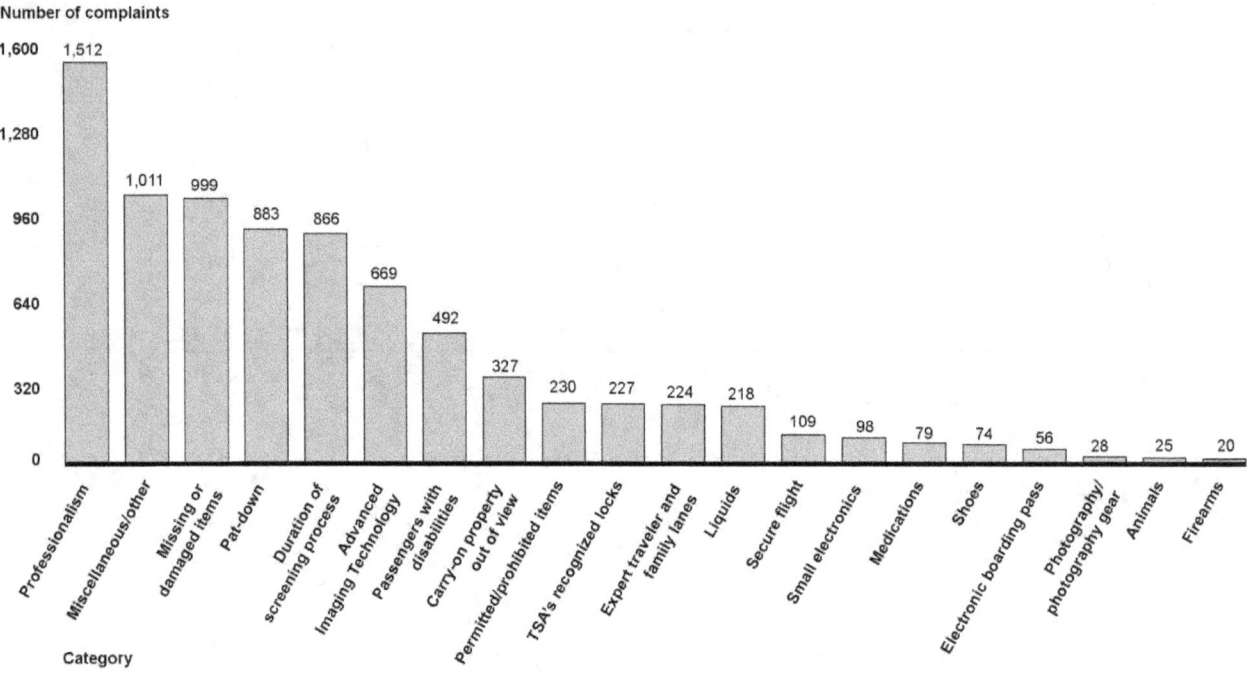

Source: GAO analysis of TSA data.

Note: When submitting complaints through this mechanism, air passengers can select up to five complaint categories from a list of 20 possible categories. If a passenger selects more than one category, each category is counted as a separate complaint when the complaints are reported by category. Thus, there are more than 4,506 complaints included in this figure. The TCC database has some categories and subcategories that are similar to the Talk to TSA categories, but others are unique to each database. For example, TCC does not have categories or subcategories corresponding to the Talk to TSA categories of carry-on property out of view, permitted/prohibited items, expert traveler and family lanes, or liquids, among others.

[34]If a passenger selects more than one category, each category is counted as a separate complaint when the complaints are reported by category. Thus, there are more than 4,506 complaints included in figure 8.

No Agencywide Policy, Consistent Processes, or Focal Point for Guiding Receipt and Use of Air Passenger Screening Complaint Information Exists

TSA has established five centralized mechanisms for receiving air passenger complaints, but it has not established an agencywide policy, consistent processes, or a focal point to guide receipt and use of this information to inform management about the nature and extent of the screening complaints to help improve screening operations and customer service.

With regard to agencywide policy, TSA has not established a policy to guide airports' efforts to receive air passenger complaints. In the absence of such a policy, TSA officials at airports have wide discretion in how they implement TSA's air passenger complaint process, including how they receive and document the complaints. For example, at the six airports that we contacted, the use of customer comment cards, which the U.S. General Services Administration (GSA) considers a relatively inexpensive means for government agencies to receive customer feedback, varied by airport.[35] Specifically, customer comment cards were not used at two of the six airports we contacted, according to TSA officials at those airports, while at the other four airports customer comment cards were used to obtain air passenger input in varying ways. At two of these four airports, customer comment cards were on display at counters in the security checkpoints. At the other two airports, neither customer comment cards nor information about the cards was on display, but the cards were available to air passengers upon request, according to TSA airport officials. Passengers who are concerned about being late for their flight or about appearing uncooperative may be reluctant to ask for such cards, however.

In addition, when TSA receives a customer comment card, either through air passengers mailing the cards, giving them to TSA screening supervisors or managers, or depositing the cards in a box at the security checkpoint, the card is to go to a customer service representative at the airport. However, TSA does not have a policy requiring that customer service representatives track these comment card submissions or report them to one of TSA's five centralized mechanisms for receiving

---

[35]TSA officials at the airports can use a TSA customer comment card to obtain feedback from air passengers. The contractor at the SPP airport we contacted uses its own customer comment card to obtain this feedback. See the website of GSA's Office of Citizen Services and Innovative Technologies for guidance on government use of customer comment cards at http://www.howto.gov/customer-service/collecting-feedback/comment-cards-fact-sheet#cost.

GAO-13-43 Air Passenger Screening Complaints

complaints if the card includes a complaint. As a result, TSA does not know the full nature and extent of the complaints that air passengers make through customer comment cards. Also, TSA officials reported that the agency does not require TSA airport staff to collect and document information on the screening complaints that air passengers submit in person at the airport level because the agency has given these officials broad discretion in addressing these screening complaints.[36] However, without an agencywide policy to guide the receipt and tracking of screening complaints at the airport level, TSA does not have reasonable assurance that headquarters and airport entities involved in the processes of receiving, tracking, and reporting these complaints are conducting these activities consistently.

Further, TSA does not have a process to use all the information it currently collects in its efforts to inform the public of the nature and extent of air passenger screening complaints, monitor air passenger satisfaction with screening operations, and identify patterns and trends in screening complaints to help improve screening operations and customer service. For example, TSA has five centralized mechanisms through which it receives air passenger complaints, but the agency does not combine information from all of these sources to analyze the full nature and extent of air passenger screening complaints. TSA officials have noted that the agency receives about 750,000 contacts per year from the public by e-mail and telephone through the TCC, and that about 8 percent of these contacts are related to complaints. However, this information does not include data on complaints received through other headquarters units or the Talk to TSA web-based form. We recognize that differences in complaint categories among the various databases could hinder any efforts by TSA to combine the complaint data, which we discuss further below.

TSA informs the public of the nature and extent of air passenger screening complaints through the U.S. Department of Transportation's monthly *Air Travel Consumer Report*, but the number TSA reports in this publication only includes complaints received through the TCC and does not include the complaints TSA received through its other four

---

[36]TSA staff at the airports we contacted told us that if air passengers make screening complaints that have the potential to attract the attention of the media, TSA screening supervisors or managers or customer service representatives would generally collect some information about the complaints in case they have to answer questions about them.

mechanisms. The July 2012 report, for example, noted that TSA had received about 900 air passenger screening complaints in May 2012, with screening complaints about courtesy and personal property constituting the bulk of the complaints and screening complaints about processing time and screening procedures constituting the rest of the complaints.[37] Further, TSA is using only the complaints received through the TCC to calculate an air passenger satisfaction indicator in its Office of Security Operations' Executive Scorecard. According to TSA, the purpose of this scorecard is for FSD management and staff to monitor operational effectiveness of airport security checkpoints and make changes as needed, such as to improve screening operations and customer service. TSA officials further stated that the agency has primarily been using the TCC because the TCC information on air passenger screening complaints is readily available. According to the Assistant Administrator of TSA's Office of Civil Rights & Liberties, Ombudsman and Traveler Engagement, partly as a result of our review, the agency began channeling information from the Talk to TSA database to the TCC in early October 2012. However, it is unclear whether the agency will compile and analyze data from the Talk to TSA database and its other centralized mechanisms in its efforts to inform the public about the nature and extent of screening complaints. It is also unclear whether these efforts will include data on screening complaints submitted locally through customer comment cards or in person at airport security checkpoints.

In addition, as discussed earlier, because TSA does not have a consistent process for categorizing air passenger complaints data, including standardized categories of complaints, it is unable to compile and analyze all of the data to identify patterns and trends. Specifically, each of the five centralized mechanisms has different screening complaint categories and different capabilities to analyze the data. As a result, TSA cannot compile information from all five mechanisms to identify patterns and trends in air passenger complaints and monitor its efforts to resolve complaints on a systemic basis. For example, while the TCC database and the Talk to TSA database each may have categories with identical or similar names, such as Advanced Imaging Technology

---

[37]U.S. Department of Transportation, Office of Aviation Enforcement and Proceedings, Aviation Consumer Protection Division, *Air Travel Consumer Report*, July 2012. The report does not define these categories of screening complaints or the extent to which these categories include information on all the categories of screening complaints in the TCC database.

GAO-13-43 Air Passenger Screening Complaints

and pat-downs, other categories are unique to certain databases. For instance, the TCC database does not have categories or subcategories corresponding to the Talk to TSA categories of carry-on property out of view, permitted/prohibited items, expert traveler and family lanes, or liquids, among others. As a result, TSA cannot combine the data from different databases to identify whether particular aspects of the screening experience may warrant additional attention or whether TSA's efforts to improve customer service are having any effect on the number of complaints.

Standards for Internal Control in the Federal Government calls for agencies to develop control activities, such as policies, procedures, techniques, and mechanisms that enforce management's directives.[38] A consistent policy to guide local TSA officials' efforts to receive, track, and report complaints would help provide TSA reasonable assurance that these activities are being conducted in a consistent manner throughout commercial airports and provide the agency with improved ability to oversee these local efforts. Moreover, a process to systematically collect information on air passenger complaints from all mechanisms, including standardization of the categories of air passenger complaints to provide a basis for comparison, would give TSA a more comprehensive picture of the volume, nature, and extent of air passenger screening complaints and better enable the agency to improve screening operations and customer service.

Further, TSA has not designated a focal point for coordinating agencywide policy and processes related to receiving, tracking, documenting, reporting, and acting on screening complaints. *Standards for Internal Control in the Federal Government* calls for an agency's organizational structure to clearly define key areas of authority and responsibility and establish appropriate lines of reporting.[39] An agencywide policy and process would help standardize how TSA receives complaints and how TSA analyzes and uses the information it collects, but without a focal point at TSA headquarters, the agency does not have a centralized entity to guide and coordinate these efforts, or to suggest any additional refinements to the system. We discuss issues related to a focal point in more detail later in this report. TSA headquarters officials we

---

[38]GAO/AIMD-00-21.3.1.

[39]GAO/AIMD-00-21.3.1.

interviewed stated that the five mechanisms were designed at different times and for different purposes, and they agreed that the agency could benefit from a consistent complaints policy, a process to collect information from all mechanisms, and a focal point to coordinate these efforts.

TSA Has Several Methods to Inform Air Passengers about Making Screening Complaints, but Does Not Consistently Implement Them

TSA has several methods to inform air passengers about its processes for making screening complaints; however, as with receipt and use of screening complaint data, it does not have an agencywide policy, guidance, and a focal point to guide these efforts, or mechanisms to share information on guidance and best practices among TSA airport staff to ensure consistency in making air passengers aware of TSA processes for submitting complaints about the screening process.

Methods at Headquarters and Airports

At the headquarters level, TSA's primary method for providing information to air passengers about TSA screening policies and processes is through the agency's website. During fiscal year 2012, TSA made improvements to its website to make it easier for air passengers to find information about how to provide feedback to TSA, including compliments and complaints, according to TSA officials. For example, the home page of TSA's website currently displays an icon that allows air passengers to ask questions or submit feedback directly to TSA staff via an electronic form. The home page also displays an icon that provides information for air passengers to contact the TCC, which receives the majority of documented air-passenger-screening-related complaints, and other TSA units involved in addressing screening complaints. At the airport level, TSA has developed several methods that local TSA staff can use to provide information at the checkpoints for air passengers to submit feedback to TSA, such as displaying signs and stickers and providing customer comment cards that contain information for contacting TSA and that allow air passengers to submit compliments and complaints.

Figure 9 shows examples of TSA's methods for informing air passengers on how to submit feedback to the agency.

Source: GAO and TSA.

Note: (A) Home page of TSA website displaying links to the electronic feedback form and contact center, (B) TSA's electronic feedback form, (C) sign placed at airport checkpoint advertising how to provide feedback to TSA, (D) stickers placed at airport checkpoints advertising TSA's electronic feedback form, (E) customer comment card drop box provided near airport checkpoint.

Inconsistent Implementation at Airports

TSA has developed standard signs, stickers, and customer comment cards that can be used at airport checkpoints to inform air passengers about how to submit feedback to the agency; however, in the absence of agencywide policy and guidance to inform air passengers, FSDs have discretion in how and whether to use these methods. As a result, there was inconsistent implementation of these methods at the six airports we contacted. For example, at one airport we visited, all four checkpoints had visible signs and stickers advertising TSA's contact information, while at another airport, we did not observe any signs or visible materials at the checkpoints advertising how to contact TSA, and at a third airport, we observed signs that were partially obscured from air passengers' view. Specifically, at one checkpoint at that third airport, we observed a sign with a quick response code for providing feedback to TSA about passengers' screening experience.[40] However, this sign was placed in a corner away from direct air passenger traffic. Also, as previously discussed, at two of six airports we contacted, customer comment cards were displayed at the checkpoint, while at two other airports customer comment cards were provided only to air passengers who specifically ask for the cards or TSA contact information or who request to speak with a screening supervisor or manager, according to TSA airport officials. As mentioned earlier, passengers who are concerned about being late for their flight or about appearing uncooperative may be reluctant to ask for such cards, however. At the remaining two airports, customer comment cards were not used, according to TSA officials at those airports. Representatives from four of the eight aviation industry groups that we interviewed also stated that the type and amount of information provided to air passengers about feedback mechanisms, such as how to submit complaints, vary among airports.

TSA airport officials we interviewed at three of the six airports we contacted stated that the agency could take additional actions to enhance air passenger awareness of TSA's complaint processes, such as posting information on shuttle buses or providing fact sheets or brochures to air passengers earlier in the screening process or during airport check-in. For example, an official at one airport suggested that TSA display audio or video materials describing TSA's complaint process, rather than posting more signs. Also, as we previously discussed, TSA's screening complaint processes entail taking corrective actions to improve screening systems, procedures, and staff. However, if air passengers wish to submit screening complaints but are not aware of the processes for doing so, air passengers may be less likely to submit complaints to the agency, thus potentially limiting the agency's efforts to identify systemic issues and take corrective actions or make any needed improvements to the screening process.

---

[40]Upon scanning the code using a smartphone, the air passenger can use the Talk to TSA electronic feedback form on TSA's website.

The Conference Report accompanying the Consolidated Appropriations Act, 2012, directed TSA to make every effort to ensure members of the traveling public are aware of the procedures and process for making complaints about passenger screening.[41] Moreover, *Standards for Internal Control in the Federal Government* states that in order to ensure effective communication to achieve agency goals, management should ensure there are adequate means of communicating with, and obtaining information from, external stakeholders that may have a significant impact on the agency's achieving its goals.[42] The standards also call for agencies to develop control activities, such as policies, procedures, techniques, and mechanisms that enforce management's directives. TSA has methods and made efforts to inform air passengers about complaint processes, but opportunities exist to increase air passenger awareness, such as through greater use of the TSA website and brochures or other materials displayed or provided at airport checkpoints, as well as through more consistent implementation of these efforts at airports. TSA officials at four of the six airports we contacted also said that the agency could do more to share best practices among customer service representatives for addressing passenger complaints, including for informing air passengers about complaint processes. For example, TSA holds periodic conference calls for Customer Support Managers to discuss customer service. However, Customer Support Managers have not used this mechanism to discuss best practices for informing air passengers about processes for submitting complaints, according to the officials we interviewed. Also, TSA has not sponsored other information-sharing mechanisms, such as training or conferences, for Customer Support Managers to learn about best practices for informing air passengers, among other things. TSA officials also recognize that passengers may intentionally choose not to submit their complaints to TSA at the airport checkpoint because of the perception that raising a complaint could result in being unfairly subjected to additional screening or being treated rudely by screening officials. In addition, TSA does not have a focal point to coordinate agencywide policy for informing air passengers about complaint processes, or to suggest additional refinements to the overall process for increasing air passenger awareness of the complaints mechanisms.

---

[41]H.R. Rep. No. 112-331, at 975 (2011).

[42]GAO/AIMD-00-21.3.1.

Accordingly, greater awareness of TSA complaint processes could help alleviate passengers' potential reluctance to submit complaints at the checkpoint. An agencywide policy to inform the public about the processes for making complaints, a focal point for developing this policy and guiding TSA's efforts to implement it, and mechanisms for sharing best practices among local TSA officials could help provide TSA reasonable assurance that these activities are being conducted in a consistent manner across commercial airports and help local TSA officials better inform the public by learning from one another about what practices work well.

TSA's Complaint Resolution Processes Lack Independence, but TSA Is Taking Steps to Increase Independence

TSA's complaint resolution processes do not fully conform to standards of independence established to help ensure that these types of processes are fair, impartial, and credible. Specifically, at the airport level, TSA officials who are responsible for resolving air passenger complaints (referred to in this report as complaint investigators) are not independent of the TSA airport staff who are the subjects of the complaints. Instead, complaint investigators are generally located in the same airport and report to the same chain of command as the individuals who are cited in the complaints. As previously discussed, TSA receives the bulk of the documented screening complaints via the TCC, and, if necessary, these complaints are ultimately investigated and resolved at the local airport level. Under TSA's process, complaints may be referred to other TSA offices, such as TSA's Disability and Multicultural Branches. These TSA branches address complaints from all air passengers with disabilities or medical conditions or from air passengers alleging violations of other civil rights or civil liberties. However, all screener-related complaints are investigated at the airport level, even for complaints that are initially referred to the Disability or Multicultural Branch.

The American Bar Association *Revised Standards for the Establishment and Operation of Ombuds Offices*, which can be used to guide federal complaint processes, states that a key indicator of independence is whether anyone subject to the ombudsman's jurisdiction can control or limit the ombudsman's performance of assigned duties.[43] Further, the

---

[43]American Bar Association, *Revised Standards for the Establishment and Operation of Ombuds Offices* (February 2004). The American Bar Association developed these standards to provide advice and guidance on the structure and operation of ombuds offices so that ombuds may better fulfill their functions and so that individuals who avail themselves of their aid may do so with greater confidence in the integrity of the process.

ombudsman is to conduct inquiries and investigations in an impartial manner, free from initial bias and conflicts of interest. Similarly, the U.S. Ombudsman Association advocates that to maintain independence, the ombudsman should have the discretion to prescribe how complaints are to be made, received, and acted upon, including the scope and manner of investigations.[44] Moreover, to ensure impartiality, the ombudsman should absent himself or herself from involvement in complaints where a conflict of interest or the appearance of conflict of interest may exist. These standards maintain that independence and impartiality are important when addressing complaints because they establish confidence that the process is fair and credible. While TSA is not required to comply with ombudsman standards, these voluntary standards can serve as a useful guideline for implementing the core principles of an effective complaint-handling process. In addition, *Standards for Internal Control in the Federal Government* states that key duties and responsibilities need to be divided or segregated among different people.[45]

At all six airports that we contacted, TSA Customer Support Managers stated that they receive air passenger complaints, review video footage of the incident, and communicate with complainants about the status and resolution of their complaints. Customer Support Managers also stated that they do not conduct formal investigations to determine the cause of a complaint or whether the screener involved in the complaint was at fault or the air passenger was misinformed. Rather, at the five airports that we contacted at which TSA has direct responsibility for screening operations, the Customer Support Managers collect information about the facts and circumstances related to the complaint and forward this information to the screener's supervisory chain.[46] At these five airports, the TSA screener supervisor or manager is responsible for obtaining the screener's statement and determining fault as well as any corrective actions that may be taken against the screener. However, TSA Customer Support

---

[44]United States Ombudsman Association, *Governmental Ombudsman Standards*, (Dayton, OH: October 2003).

[45]GAO/AIMD-00-21.3.1.

[46]At the SPP airport that we contacted, the TSA Customer Support Manager is responsible for addressing screening complaints related to policy and standard operating procedures. The contractor is responsible for collecting information about the facts and circumstances related to complaints about a passenger's screening experience as well as resolving these complaints or, if necessary, referring them to TSA for resolution.

Managers as well as all TSA screening personnel, including TSA screening supervisors and managers, report to FSDs, and are therefore in the same chain of command as the subjects of air passenger complaints. Because FSDs may be concerned about complaints reflecting negatively on their management of TSA screening operations, this raises questions about independence and the appearance of impartiality and their ability to conduct credible, unbiased investigations. Figure 10 depicts a simplified example of the typical reporting structure at airports at which TSA has direct responsibility for screening operations.

Figure 10: Simplified Organizational Chart Depicting TSA Chain of Command at a Typical Category X Airport

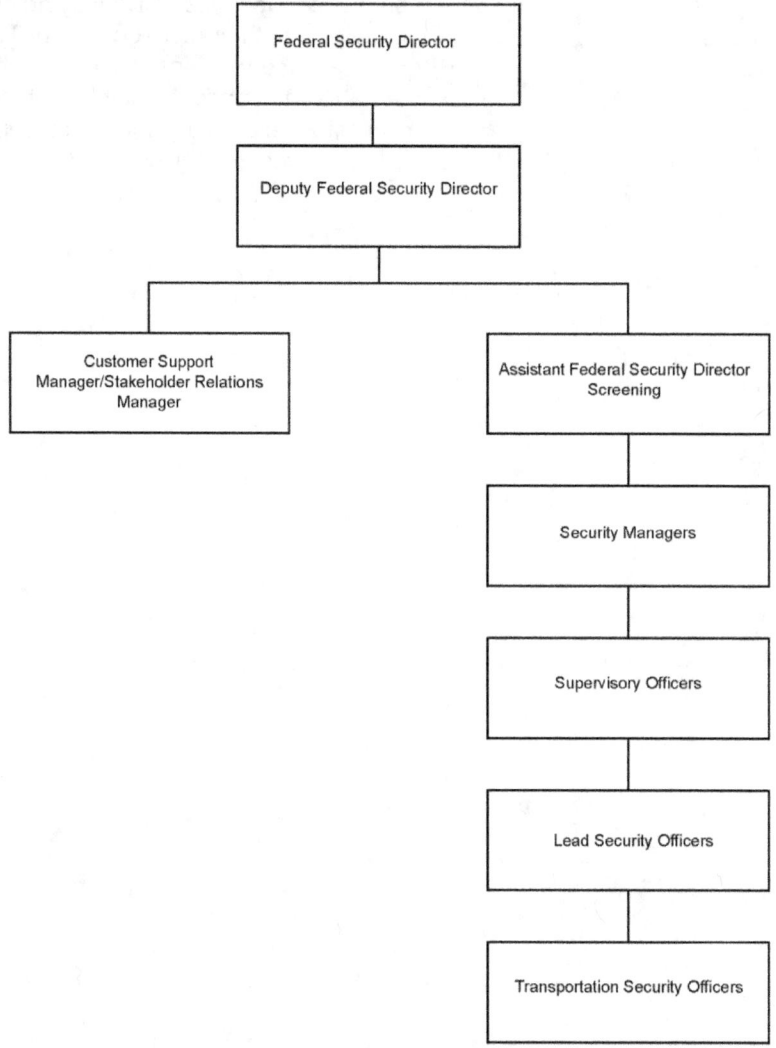

Source: GAO analysis of TSA information.

Note: According to TSA officials, the Customer Support Managers and Stakeholder Relations Managers can report directly to the FSD, to the Deputy FSD, to the AFSD for Screening, to the AFSD for Operations, or to the AFSD for Mission Support depending on the airport. TSA classifies commercial airports into one of five categories (X, I, II, III, and IV) based on various factors, such as the total number of takeoffs and landings annually, the extent to which passengers are screened at the airport, and other special security considerations. In general, category X airports have the largest number of passenger boardings, and category IV airports have the smallest.

TSA officials stated that the desire to resolve complaints locally led to TSA's decision to allow complaint investigators to be located in the same airport with those whom they are investigating. Also, TSA officials noted that resource constraints may limit the agency's ability to send TSA officials from headquarters offices to conduct independent investigations of complaints at each airport. However, the lack of independence of the complaint investigators creates the potential for a conflict of interest to arise between the investigator and the individual under investigation. For this reason, in accordance with ombudsman standards, it is important for the structure of the complaint process to ensure the independence of complaint investigators in order to maintain impartial investigations, as well as to maintain the appearance of impartiality during investigations, not only to ensure that they are being fair, but also to uphold the credibility of the complaint process. Having a more independent complaint resolution process would better position TSA to make informed and unbiased decisions about complaints and ensure that corrective actions are taken, as needed, against screeners who are reported to have exhibited unprofessional or inappropriate behavior with air passengers.

While TSA has an Ombudsman Division that could help ensure greater independence in the complaint processes, it primarily focuses on handling internal personnel matters and is not yet fully equipped to address external complaints from air passengers, according to the head of that division. However, recognizing the importance of independence in the complaint processes, TSA is developing a new process for referring air passenger complaints directly to this office from airports and for providing air passengers an independent avenue to make complaints about airport checkpoint screening. In August 2012, during the course of our review, TSA's Ombudsman Division began addressing a small number of air passenger complaints forwarded from the TCC, according to the head of that division. TSA also began advertising the division's new role in addressing passenger screening complaints via the TSA website in October 2012. The Assistant Administrator of TSA's Office of Civil Rights & Liberties, Ombudsman and Traveler Engagement stated that she expected the Ombudsman Division to begin addressing a greater number of air passenger complaints as a result. According to the Assistant Administrator, the division will not handle complaints for which there exists an established process that includes an appeal function, such as disability complaints or other civil rights or civil liberties complaints, in order to avoid duplication of currently established processes. Since the external function of the Ombudsman Division has not yet been fully implemented, it is too early to assess the extent to which this new function of the complaints resolution process will conform to professional standards for organizational independence, and help mitigate possible concerns about impartiality and objectivity.

TSA is also in the process of developing a Passenger Advocate Program, which the agency plans to begin implementing by January 2013, according to the Assistant Administrator of TSA's Office of Civil Rights & Liberties, Ombudsman and Traveler Engagement. This program will entail training selected TSA airport staff to take on a collateral passenger advocate role, according to that official. Passenger advocates will respond in real time to identify and resolve traveler-related screening complaints quickly, consistent with TSA policies and screening procedures, according to the Assistant Administrator. Advocates will also respond to air passenger requests, assist air passengers with medical conditions or disabilities, and be prepared to assist air passengers who provide advance notification to TSA via the national TSA Cares helpline. According to the Assistant Administrator, the Passenger Advocate Program will work in conjunction with the new external complaint function of the Ombudsman Division and provide air passenger advocates with the option to refer air passengers directly to the Ombudsman Division. Because passenger advocates are to serve under the FSD chain of command, this arrangement also raises questions about whether there is a lack of independence between passenger advocates and the subjects of air passenger complaints. The Assistant Administrator explained that any perception of lack of independence would be addressed by training passenger advocates to explain to air passengers that they may submit complaints directly to the Ombudsman, who is outside of the airport chain of command. Because this program has not yet been approved by the TSA Administrator or implemented, it is too early to assess the extent to which passenger advocates will help mitigate possible concerns about impartiality and objectivity in the complaint processes.

Conclusions

According to available data, TSA receives a relatively small number of complaints considering the millions of air passengers the agency screens each month. However, the agency's ability to understand the full nature and extent of those complaints is limited because TSA does not systematically collect some of the screening complaint data at the airport level, uses only some of the data it has available to it in its reports and analysis, and collects the data in a manner that makes it difficult for the agency to aggregate and analyze the data for trends. Further, the inconsistent nature of implementation of the screening complaint processes at commercial airports limits TSA's ability to oversee these efforts. Thus, a policy to consistently guide agencywide efforts to receive, track, and report air passenger screening complaints would help provide TSA reasonable assurance that TSA headquarters and airport entities are conducting these activities consistently. Moreover, a consistent process to systematically analyze information on air passenger screening complaints from all mechanisms for receiving complaints, including standardized screening complaint categories and capabilities for data analysis, would give TSA a more comprehensive picture of the volume, nature, and extent of air passenger screening complaints and better enable the agency to improve screening operations and customer service. In addition, designating a focal point for developing and coordinating agencywide policy on air passenger screening complaint processes, guiding the analysis and use of the agency's screening complaint data, and informing the public about the nature and extent of screening complaints would help ensure that these efforts are implemented consistently throughout the agency. Finally, TSA has a number of methods to inform the public about its processes for submitting screening complaints, but does not have an agencywide policy to guide these efforts or mechanisms for sharing best practices for informing air passengers about screening complaint processes, which could help TSA staff—particularly at the airport level—better inform the public by learning from one another about what is working well.

Recommendations for Executive Action

To improve TSA's oversight of air passenger screening complaint processes, we recommend that the Administrator of TSA take the following four actions, consistent with standards for internal control, to

- establish a consistent policy to guide agencywide efforts for receiving, tracking, and reporting air passenger screening complaints;
- establish a process to systematically compile and analyze information on air passenger screening complaints from all complaint mechanisms;
- designate a focal point to develop and coordinate agencywide policy on screening complaint processes, guide the analysis and use of the agency's screening complaint data, and inform the public about the nature and extent of screening complaints; and
- establish agencywide policy to guide TSA's efforts to inform air passengers about the screening complaint processes and establish mechanisms, particularly at the airport level, to share information on best practices for informing air passengers about the screening complaint processes.

Agency Comments and Our Evaluation

We provided a draft of this report to the Department of Homeland Security (DHS) for comment. DHS, in written comments received October 16, 2012, concurred with the recommendations and identified actions taken, under way, or planned to implement the recommendations. Written comments are summarized below, and official DHS comments are reproduced in appendix I. In addition, DHS provided written technical comments, which we incorporated, as appropriate.

In response to our recommendation that TSA establish a consistent policy to guide agencywide efforts for receiving, tracking, and reporting air passenger screening complaints, DHS concurred with the recommendation and stated that TSA would review current intake and processing procedures at headquarters and in the field and develop policy, as appropriate, to better guide the efforts of headquarters and field locations in receiving, tracking, and reporting air passenger screening complaints. We believe that these are beneficial steps that would address our recommendation, provided that the resulting policy refinements improve the existing processes for receiving, tracking, and reporting all air passenger screening complaints, including the screening complaints that air passengers submit locally at airports through comment cards or in person at security checkpoints.

In response to our recommendation that TSA establish a process to systematically compile and analyze information on air passenger screening complaints from all complaint mechanisms, DHS concurred with the recommendation and stated that TSA, through the TCC, is taking steps to increase its analysis of passenger complaint information and will build on this effort to further compile and analyze information on air passenger screening complaints. However, DHS did not provide additional details on the steps TSA is taking, so we cannot comment on the extent to which these steps will fully address our recommendation. In its technical comments, TSA stated that the agency began channeling information from the Talk to TSA database to the TCC on October 3, 2012, and we updated our report accordingly. However, it is still unclear whether TSA will compile and analyze data from the Talk to TSA database and its other centralized mechanisms in its efforts to inform the public about the nature and extent of screening complaints and whether these efforts will include data on screening complaints submitted locally at airports through customer comment cards or in person at airport security checkpoints. It is also unclear how TSA will address the difficulties we identified in collecting standardized screening data across different complaint categories and mechanisms. As highlighted in our report, establishing a consistent process to systematically compile and analyze information on air passenger screening complaints will help provide TSA with a more comprehensive picture of the volume, nature, and extent of air passenger screening complaints and better enable the agency to improve screening operations and customer service for the traveling public.

In response to our recommendation that TSA designate a focal point for the complaints identification, analysis, and public outreach process, DHS concurred with the recommendation and stated that the Assistant Administrator for the Office of Civil Rights & Liberties, Ombudsman and Traveler Engagement is the focal point for overseeing the key TSA entities involved with processing passenger screening complaints. We are encouraged that the agency has identified a focal point for these efforts but note that the Assistant Administrator only oversees the TSA's complaint-related processes in the Office of Civil Rights & Liberties, Ombudsman and Traveler Engagement. Thus, it will be important for the Assistant Administrator to coordinate with other TSA offices when acting as the TSA focal point to address the weaknesses we identified in our report. For example, as mentioned in DHS's comment letter, it will be important for the Assistant Administrator to work closely with the office of the Assistant Administrator of Security Operations because this office oversees screening operations at commercial airports and security operations staff in the field who receive screening complaints submitted through customer comment cards or in person at airport security checkpoints. The Assistant Administrator for the Office of Civil Rights & Liberties, Ombudsman and Traveler Engagement will also need to coordinate with the Office of the Executive Secretariat, which is not mentioned in DHS's comment letter, given the thousands of air passenger complaints that this office receives, as well as with other DHS and TSA offices that have a role in the air passenger complaint processes—including, but not limited to, the TSA Office of Inspections, TSA Office of Legislative Affairs, and the DHS Office of the Inspector General.

In response to our recommendation that TSA establish agencywide policy to guide TSA's efforts to inform air passengers about the screening complaint processes and establish mechanisms, particularly at the airport level, to share information on best practices for informing air passengers about the screening complaint processes, DHS concurred with the recommendation. DHS stated that TSA would develop a policy to better inform air passengers about the screening complaint processes, to include mechanisms for identifying and sharing best practices for implementing these processes at the airport level. We will continue to monitor TSA's progress in implementing this recommendation.

We are sending copies of this report to the Secretary of Homeland Security, the TSA Administrator, appropriate congressional committees, and other interested parties. In addition, the report is available at no charge on the GAO website at http://www.gao.gov.

If you or your staff have any questions concerning this report, please contact me at (202) 512-4379 or at lords@gao.gov. Contact points for our Offices of Congressional Relations and Public Affairs may be found on that last page of this report. GAO staff who made major contributions to this report are listed in appendix II.

Stephen M. Lord
Director
Homeland Security and Justice Issues

List of Committees

The Honorable Mary Landrieu
Chairman
The Honorable Dan Coats
Ranking Member
Subcommittee on Homeland Security
Committee on Appropriations
United States Senate

The Honorable Robert B. Aderholt
Chairman
The Honorable David E. Price
Ranking Member
Subcommittee on Homeland Security
Committee on Appropriations
House of Representatives

Appendix I: Comments from the Department of Homeland Security

U.S. Department of Homeland Security
Washington, DC 20528

Homeland Security

October 16, 2012

Stephen M. Lord
Director, Homeland Security and Justice Issues
U.S. Government Accountability Office
441 G Street, NW
Washington, DC 20548

Re: GAO Draft Report 13-43, "AIR PASSENGER SCREENING: Transportation Security
  Administration Could Improve Complaint Processes"

Dear Mr. Lord:

Thank you for the opportunity to review and comment on this draft report. The U.S. Department
of Homeland Security (DHS) appreciates the U.S. Government Accountability Office's (GAO's)
work in planning and conducting its review and issuing this report.

The Department is pleased to note GAO's recognition that the Transportation Security
Administration (TSA) (1) screens some 650 million passengers a year, and (2) currently has
complaint processes in place and has made efforts to inform air passengers about them. TSA
strives to provide the highest level of security while ensuring that all passengers are treated with
dignity and respect. The agency works regularly with a broad coalition of disability and medical
condition advocacy groups to help understand their needs and adapt screening procedures
accordingly.

While the majority of passengers approve of TSA's handling of security screening,[1] TSA takes
all complaints seriously. Accordingly, TSA has several initiatives underway to systematically
collect, analyze, report, and share screening complaint data. TSA also continues to explore other
avenues to leverage current resources, such as greater use of TSA's Web site and more consistent
use of brochures and materials displayed or provided at airport checkpoints. Additionally, in
December 2011, TSA launched "TSA Cares," a new helpline available 24 hours per day,
designed to assist travelers with disabilities and medical conditions prior to getting to the
airport. When a passenger with a disability or medical condition calls TSA Cares, a
representative will assist, either by providing information about screening that is relevant to the
passenger's specific disability or medical condition or by referring the passenger to disability
experts at TSA.

TSA is also creating a Passenger Advocate Program to augment TSA Stakeholder Managers and
Customer Support and Quality Improvement Managers by establishing collateral-duty passenger
advocates who will respond in "real time" to identify and quickly resolve traveler-related

---

[1] http://www.gallup.com/poll/156491/Americans-Views-TSA-Positive-Negative.aspx

screening complaints, consistent with TSA policies and screening procedures. Further, TSA will continue to take steps to share information on best practices among airports and to provide information to the traveling public on how TSA handles passenger issues and complaints.

The draft report contained four recommendations with which DHS concurs. Specifically, GAO recommended the Administrator of TSA:

Recommendation 1: Establish a consistent policy to guide agency wide efforts for receiving, tracking, and reporting air passenger screening complaints.

Response: Concur. TSA, through the TSA Contact Center (TCC), has already taken steps to receive and refer complaints to offices dealing with disability, medical, and civil rights issues, and review feedback from the *Talk to TSA* Web link. TSA will review current intake and processing procedures at Headquarters and the field and develop policy, as appropriate, to better guide the efforts of Headquarters and field locations in receiving, tracking, and reporting air passenger screening complaints.

Recommendation 2: Establish a process to systematically compile and analyze information on air passenger screening complaints from all complaint mechanisms.

Response: Concur. TSA, through the TCC, is taking steps to increase its analysis of passenger complaint information and will build on this effort to further compile and analyze information on air passenger screening complaints.

Recommendation 3: Designate a focal point to develop and coordinate agency wide policy on screening complaint processes, guide the analysis and use of the agency's screening complaint data, and inform the public about the nature and extent of screening complaints.

Response: Concur. The Assistant Administrator for the Office of Civil Rights & Liberties, Ombudsman, and Traveler Engagement has the primary responsibility for, and is the focal point for, overseeing the key TSA entities involved with processing passenger screening complaints. The office includes the Traveler Engagement Division (with the TCC); the Disability and Multicultural Division (with the Disability Branch and the Multicultural Branch); and the Ombudsman Division. In addition, the Assistant Administrator will improve coordination with the Office of Security Operations regarding passenger screening procedures and the Office of Public Affairs to develop and share data with the public on passenger complaint screening processes.

Recommendation 4: Establish agency wide policy to guide TSA's efforts to inform air passengers about the screening complaint processes and establish mechanisms, particularly at the airport level, to share information on best practices for informing air passengers about the screening complaint processes.

2

Response: Concur. TSA will develop a policy to better inform air passengers about the screening complaint processes, including mechanisms for identifying and sharing best practices for implementing these processes at the airport level.

Again, thank you for the opportunity to review and comment on this draft report. Technical comments were previously provided under separate cover. Please feel free to contact me if you have any questions. We look forward to working with you in the future.

Sincerely,

Jim H. Crumpacker
Director
Departmental GAO-OIG Liaison Office

3

Appendix II: GAO Contact and Staff Acknowledgments

GAO Contact	Stephen M. Lord, (202) 512-4379 or lords@gao.gov
Staff Acknowledgments	In addition to the contact named above, Jessica Lucas-Judy (Assistant Director), Carissa Bryant, and Juan Tapia-Videla made significant contributions to the work. Also contributing to this report were David Alexander, Lydia Araya, Tom Lombardi, Lara Miklozek, and Linda Miller.

www.ingramcontent.com/pod-product-compliance
Lightning Source LLC
Chambersburg PA
CBHW080613290526
45790CB00007B/2761